Reading the Earth

Reading the Earth

Poems by
Claude Wilkinson

Michigan State University Press
East Lansing

∞ The paper used in this publication meets the minimum require-
ments of ANSI/NISO Z39.48-1992 (R 1997) (Permanence of Paper).

Michigan State University Press
East Lansing, Michigan 48823-5202

03 02 01 00 99 98   1 2 3 4 5 6 7 8

Library of Congress Cataloging-in-Publication Data

Wilkinson, Claude.
    Reading the Earth : poems / by Claude Wilkinson
        p.   cm. — (Lotus Poetry Series)
    ISBN 0-87013-481-7 (alk. paper)
    I. Title. II. Series.
    PS3573.I44183R42   1998
    811'.54—dc21   98-22066
                                                            CIP

Lotus Poetry Series Editor: Naomi Long Madgett

Acknowledgments

The author wishes to thank the editors of the following magazines in which some of these poems previously appeared:

Albatross: "Moles"
A New Song: "Knell," "Reading the Earth," "Way of Life,"
   "White Horses"
Atlanta Review: "Baptism with Water Moccasin," "God's Acre"
Blue Mesa Review: "Savanna"
California State Poetry Quarterly: "Hummingbirds"
Connecticut River Review: "Lively Oracles"
DeKalb Literary Arts Journal: "Juke"
Grasslands Review: "Expecting Blackbirds"
Number One: "Driving," "Landmarks," "Marigolds," "Mowing the
   Lawn," "On My Sister's Wedding"
Old Hickory Review: "Shells"
Poem: "A Simpler Optimism," "Blackberry Fools," "By Night,"
   "Ephemerida," "Epoch," "Fall Song"
Reflections: "Hernando Point," "Natchez Trace"
Roanoke Review: "Firelight"
Sunrust: "The Men's Club Hunt"
The North Mississippi Herald: "The Christ's-thorn"
Visions International: "Ceremony"
Voices International: "Whippoorwill"
Wind: "Evanescence," "Raking Leaves"
Windhover: "Slug"
Writers on the River: "Bobwhites on a Spring Morning"

Consider the lilies how they grow:
they toil not, they spin not;
and yet I say unto you,
that Solomon in all his glory
was not arrayed like one of these.
— *Luke 12:27*

Contents

Driving   1
Expecting Blackbirds   2
Reading the Earth   3
The Christ's-thorn   5
Knell   7
The Rattlesnake — Contemplations on a Bronze
   by Frederick Remington   10
Hummingbirds   14
On My Sister's Wedding   15
Borrowed Time   16
Slug   18
By Night   19
Bobwhites on a Spring Morning   20
Act of God   21
Whitetail   23
Shells   24
Baptism with Water Moccasin   26
White Horses   28
Whippoorwill   31
Juke   33
Marigolds   35
June   38
Midsummer   40
Haute Cuisine   41
Mowing the Lawn   43
Ceremony   46
Moles   47
Fall Song   48
Hernando Point   49
Lively Oracles   50
Blackberry Fools   51
Epoch   53

Raking Leaves   54
The Men's Club Hunt   55
Firelight   57
Landmarks   58
Evanescence   59
Natchez Trace   60
The Falcon   61
God's Acre   62
A Simpler Optimism   64
Savanna   65
Ephemerida   66
Way of Life   70
Dealate   72

About the Author   75

Driving

Sometimes by the wayside, there's a shack
tottering from age and decay, its chinks
sifting the moonlight, filling with dock
and cocklebur, a lane you feel you've traveled
though you've never driven this route before.

In the few seconds it takes to pass,
a twinge shivers through your halfheartedness
that's being kept between dashes and stripes
only by the zoom of oncoming headlights.
For no earthly reason, you want to stop

and leave the car, to slip down
the glistening shoulder and wade through
the sea of soybeans or cotton, creak
gingerly onto the porch where
a sharecropper must've sat at least once

on some hot twinkling night
and wept over wife or drought, then
to ease inside where love was made up
time and again to the cadence
of whippoorwills and crickets.

Yet, if for nothing other than the comfort
of your fingers around a steering wheel,
the hypnotic pulse of tires, you keep
humming along, holding course,
reading stories as fleet as ghosts.

Expecting Blackbirds

Except for the change
in the colors
of the world,
you won't be warned
of their coming.

All morning
glistening black bands
will freckle the air,
load their chatter
on baring trees.

They'll burn hours
drove-darting pinnacles:
fence posts, fence wires —
filing their contempt
for lumber, old tires,
whatever hesitates below.

Like clockwork they'll rise
from cattails and clover,
from every dark field
to camp about their Jericho
and shout down
our forts of quiet.

Reading the Earth

Through ribbons of berylline leaves
my pruning shears crisscrossed,
snipping wayward limbs,
restoring a willow's canopy
till they snarled in the neat funnel
of twigs that was a bird's nest.

Even without its pearl of eggs
it glowed like a mandorla
in the pageant of twilight.
What one could so easily miss though
are the nuggets of gum foil
twisted and crimped as carefully
as origami, that perfectly laced
pastiche of spider web and thistle,
a silver godsend of snakeskin
lining it like smithery,
all firmly mortised
in the willow's most likely fork.

For whatever reason —
call it psychometry or haruspicy,
but as the nest became a revelation of fire,
I thought of Ezekiel's vision of God
along the Chebar: those jeweled wheels,
the lightning and flame, winged creatures
darting back and forth
at the hub of the sky,
the center of his calling
to be Israel's watchman
and warn the people
when they went astray.

Some nights before on TV,
there was this environmentalist railing,
"To hell with the Bible,"
quoting some brother fanatic who'd said,
"We should put it away
for the next twenty years
and start reading the earth."

Once I heard a preacher
paraphrasing Luke, saying,
"You never see a sparrow
in the unemployment line,"
 meaning not just that even
the simplest of souls
relied on some master plan,
a design beyond their own, but
perhaps also, that in their simplicity
grace was more complete.

In the lush silence
I thought of Noah who'd become
history's ultimate conservationist
going on nothing but a voice,
how the Ark near the end must've been
an asylum of daws and kookaburras,
its rafters molting a feathered palette
of golds, scarlets and indigos,
yet it's difficult to imagine any of them,
even Darwin's finches, chiming,
"What's in a faith?" having been
at the heart of that grand a plot
and only praising such a small part.

The Christ's-thorn

Only a cloud
of garnet spines, a *cheval-de-frise*
at the edge of the yard,
but what a wonder
to witness cardinals and kinglets
alighting in it,
the polished rosaries of their eyes
as generous as stained glass.

For them, peril
has no such face: the thorn
is rest, above
the crossroads of sky,
elsewhere is a destination
they will or won't undertake.

They wouldn't dream of
injury from such convenience
pricking their crests,
the bright nimbus of blood
it could draw.

It's anguish to finger, even to think of,
the hard cockspur,
and yet I've had to fight my hands
twisting the twigs, fashioning them,
testing if you wish,
their legend of suppleness

till the air of muted singing
becomes urgent enough
to resurrect one

to things of this life, back
to thorny branches
where all the sacred birds
have alas taken off.

Knell

When we thought
we might've had Mama back
from all the chemo and surgeries,
the specialists who'd begun speaking
in soft, uncommitted ways,
from the medieval bleedings
by each shift of nurses
till her veins became of no use,
till hands that had guided our hands
through difficult vectors and loops of alphabet
now had to be steadied themselves
to scrawl the hospital's ream of forms,
from her dwindling frame
being riddled with tubes,
that prison of bedpans —

never back to the strength
for kneading pie dough,
to the one who'd basted
and hemstitched our clothes,
who'd been expert at twisting off
a fryer's head or sugar-crusted preserve lids,
who was constantly the mother of invention
for our needs — but at least
saved from all that,

I sat alone in darkness
on the floor all night
unable to weep or worship
or even to adore the sky,
unwilling to allow any part of her miracle
outside myself before it could also heal

the wasteland I'd become
over the years of sackcloth and fasting,
desperate to strike some bargain with God.

When her health reversed
after a few months, skidded
so quickly into that numbing report,
it hadn't left time
to fear a ringing phone again —
only the pale quiet of afternoon,
a lush coasting of snow.

Who can say how years later
some moonstruck toad enters this picture?
Yet, one evening
when I'd gone out for the mail,
there it was hopping hell-bent
toward rush-hour traffic.

Turning away after
having shooed him back to safety
no less than twice, I saw him
angle himself again for the other side.

And for what?
Had there been trilling
of some starlit pond
beyond the black slope of pines
where moths or melon flies
hover gloriously for the tongue?

When a UPS van shot past,
then a couple more cars
miraculously straddled him,
I focused on a neighbor's house
lit like a great hall
among the dark, distant stands, on
the holy spice of sassafras.

It wasn't till the silver Chrysler
that his sober toll,
like a plump maypop being stomped,
set the nausea of doubt
churning once more, sent its raw echo
surging through this life again,
interrupting rich breaths of loam
though planets maintained their glistening
alignment, though heaven was frozen
as high as ever,
and the tiny ruffle of innards
already turning to stone.

The Rattlesnake — **Contemplations on a Bronze**
by Frederick Remington

Over the rope
of gallery gibberish
I heard one lady say,
"The snake should be coiled."
Obviously the snake's repose
captivated her more
than the skillful striations
in the horse's mane,
the rugged execution
of the rider's chaps.

It was that old phobia again —
where every snake
is looped in our minds,
always ready to prick us
with a bit more pain.

Overshadowing her pleasure
for the brilliant bucking,
any concerns about
whether the cowboy is thrown
or whether the rattler
even strikes is
that inescapable word
that God cursed serpents
beyond everything else.

Lost in the perfect crook
of the horse's shank,
the startling reverence
of his eyes,

I also wrestled through
problems of whether
the artist had begun
with the snake
or if it had simply
wriggled its way in
once again to the heart
of a scene, found myself
wondering how horses,
so full of majesty and thunder,
came to fear
something so lowly.

Yet, my grandfather,
who'd been virile enough
to make and feed thirteen mouths,
died quietly one day
after work in the fields.
My mother said
they'd found two pinholes
between his ankle and calf.

From the crimson flowering
and swelling, the way
he'd faded so magically
after his noonday meal,
they finally settled
on snakebite as the cause.

And once she told me of
how, one bright summer morning
while she was sitting on the porch,
a blue racer
had sped through
our unmowed grass,
hissed and leaped
high into the air
right in front of her
till she stiffened with fear.
So from then on, she wanted
all of them killed.

From then on,
we children waited
on their length
after the first jonquils,
knocked them out of trees,
smashed them with shovels,
hacked them with hoes
till their glistening innards
flowed like crushed stars.

We watched with a joy
something like madness
as they writhed
from pulped heads,
their dark blood
coating ages of dust
with the same rich patina
creeping over this cast.

What Remington's horse
must feel are generations
of whinnying being uttered
from that first wild mother
that had watched her foal
or mate trip
numbly into clover
after trotting too near
a poisoned lash,
the evil connection
between snakes and loss
now firmly at his heels.

Hummingbirds

Almost bee, almost bird,
almost fairy, almost flower
whirring in on an ounce of air,
a hundred times I've missed
their emerald, amethyst, ruby arrivals.

In a spell
they're there like iridescent puppets
as steady as spring, hung
before the hottest red trumpets
for that sultry kiss of nectar,

their bills and tongues
a harmony of swizzle sticks
among the anthers and pistils.
How often they have to splash
and pivot from blossom to blossom

to feed, just to feed,
just to be alive.
Even over into the night,
I feel their tiny hearts
humming like love —

always crying to get deeper and sweeter,
almost see them
only lightly sleeping, dreaming
nothing but red: the color
of all desire.

On My Sister's Wedding

Barely six years of blood
separated us, what we picked up
of Tumblins and Gambles
and the lot of odd yarns
that peopled Mama's tongue.

Up front before God again,
this time beyond the mourners' bench,
she may be smiling inside
over the elders' spooky salvations
of walking 'cross hell on a spider web
or perhaps retasting
her first choice of treats.

Perhaps she was past that, to where
the years had resolved nip and tuck
into something bearable at last,
at our secret heap
where I was taught how to choose
from the spectrum of bottles
by the big sister dogmas
of brilliance and design;

or past that even, to the trifles
of rice at the sanctuary door
where we hug and part,
where she leaves *us*,
to be the flesh of another.

Borrowed Time

Mega-tortoise wins race with death
as $89.89 purchase saves its neck
— *The Commercial Appeal*

Of all things,
a Cadillac salesman
had spared him this time
from being diced up and sold
by the pound. I won't forget
his looking so old and annoyed
as a couple of zoologists
heaved him, breech end first,
into the bed of their truck,
hungry for the secrets
from his hundred plus years.

How incensed he must've been
at fishermen who'd stripped him
from the slimy emerald
of his bayou
even as that mace of a body
lashed through cool rafts
of lotus and duckweed,
how furious at
the cheeky reporter
who, with one dazzling flash,
exposed him hoisted
to this limbo
between heaven and earth,

both huge Jurassic foreclaws
lolling like plumb bobs
over the tailgate,
those enemy jaws
gaping at the thought
of locking on any one
of these traitors
till thunder freed them,
hissing to get hold
and munch off their heads
as he'd already done those
two whippersnapper snappers
that some crazy fishmonger
had dared put
in the same tank.

After all, how was he to know
that he was being passed
from death unto life,
that after a few days' study
he'd again be idling
in the carol of loons,
issuant once more
in some wide ripple of water,
waiting like a trap door
for goslings and carp,
left for awhile longer
to his chronic thanatopsis —
oblivious of how many
such kindnesses have kept
him out of the soup.

Slug

How is it that even through the pitch-black lawn
    and drizzle as awesome
as a typhoon for you, the gauntlet of night beaks
    for which you would
be simply greasy ambrosia, that you, without so
    much as one decent
eye, and no other visible guide but the map of
    your diaphanous lust,
can manage to lube a way onto my porch to take
    what the dog has left?
Anyhow, perhaps it was that slow bulging of horns
    as you dribbled into
the orgy of scraps — those horns, and your rising
    from damp waves
of grass that likened you to evil, the beast of
    Revelation that will
come from the sea. Perhaps it was because you
    were my only
real chance to prove the philosophy of resisting
    sin, be the salt
I'm supposed to be, that I squandered a few grains
    and marveled
at how you dwindled like lightning from both ends
    at once.

By Night

Some nights it's impossible
        to imagine the Fall.
                Angels are so close
that the owls are awed.
        Orphic lights
                swirl above as if
in a burst of van Gogh.
        The hum in the cedars
                is something like sleep.
We sit and dream
        of the gone day,
                how a hawk carved wheels
in the sky
        till bullbats swoop
                too near the hush,
shatter us back
        to where another revolution
                is singly subtracting the stars.

Bobwhites on a Spring Morning

A bobwhite sounds through larks
and jays, the wringing-wet shade,
as in the first world, before Adam
understood their sharp iambs,
when the refrain could've been
anything's: plant or animal, or light
so pure it sang. Even now
how absolute, how wondrously
primitive the singularity rings —
shouting its name, its name,
its name . . . till from elsewhere
an echo swells through April-thick wings
as if addressing some question
on the presence of parallels.

Act of God

All morning the heavens
had been filling with
torrents of violet rain, rows
of cottonwood and willow so lashed by wind
they resembled the bowlike palms
in a watercolor titled *Bahamian Scene*,
of which I remembered being especially fond —

partly because of the way the painter
had splashed light across the paper,
illuminating edges and interiors of clouds,
but mainly because of the beauty
in fear so obvious there at that spit
of beach with a few desperate schooners
visible in the distance but far
too far from home, a family
snatching up what's likely
the day's harvest of shells or fish
toward the hope of a hut buttressed with roses,
in the couple of freewheeling gulls
caught so starkly white between
the painting's slate-blue sky
and its restless swells of ultramarine.

For instance, I know how once
the family's inside, children will be
warned not to peek out and made to avoid
all youthful silliness as if
in reverence to some tantrum of nature, how
everyone will all huddle together
in one dark room, praying now and then
till it all blows over, adults

miming to each other only
the most necessary things,
how the kids will be near bursting
at the seams from the rare intensity
of this bond, their new sense of life
welling to goose flesh under clatter
of thunder and whistling fronds.

And when fury at last changes
into its usual wondrous horizon
of iridescent bands, and stories
begin filing in about twisters
that rumbled through like freight trains,
of a neighbor's roof being shorn
clean off, the old bell tower
scorched by lightning, I know how
absolutely blessed each breath will feel
in the litter of petals and fallen limbs,
when the first ruffled birds
start whirling and chiming
as if they'd just been born.

Whitetail

Stark out of nowhere
  springing down the rush
    of the bank — quickly to eclipse
      the ash-colored rains
clotting above
  and greens as loud
    as those made by a child,
      the two redwings
I'd spotted
  a little while back —
    and onto the orange road.
      First I thought of salt. Then
there was this time in Louisiana
  when I saw a man's head
    among the clouds —
      nothing as white as its plume.
But then, buck, and up
  a lush west slope
    to stash once more
      at the root of the world.

Shells

Her whole living room
was an amazement of trinkets:
the smiling Maharajah bank
whose head bobbed "yes"
like a temple dancer;
the arrogant ceramic tabby
that coiled on the narrow hearth
between a small gas heater
and my uncle's recliner;
a fat clay goose
and her two cartoonish goslings
that never waddled
from under the mantle,
never once crossed
the parquet lake.

Across the room, every inch
of her washstand was crowded
with tawny chronicles of relatives
posed like vanguards in zoot suits
or doughboy gear,
ready on all fronts
to jitterbug or invade.

Of all these, the shells
were my favorite,
the only items of her house
that weren't in dotage.
I loved the ways
they frilled and scalloped
into purple and specks,
their tranquil memory of waves.

But it was often Sunday
before I could filch
their distant songs —
when Grandma was engrossed
in her radio preachers.
Even then, sometimes
when I'd chosen a shell,
I'd hear her calling out
from her mahogany rocker
in another room,
gently denying me
the pleasure of the sea.

Baptism with Water Moccasin

And the Lord said to Satan, "From where do you come?" So
Satan answered the Lord and said, "From going to and fro on
the earth, and from walking back and forth on it."

— *The Book of Job*

His bulk amazed us,
the way he'd maneuvered his folds
onto a switch of elm
directly above the baptizing hole.
After all, Cedar Creek offered
numerous spots for a snake
to wile away a Sunday, but only one
fit to baptize in.

Not even the brilliance
of proselytes, a rite of sheets
fluttering about them
in the early morning breeze,
had moved him. Not the most
floral, feathered, tasseled of hats,
nor the highest notes of a Doctor Watt
being held till the last thread
of their power —
nothing made him so much
as shift that bitter lozenge of head,
shovel through the chilly fork of his tongue
to even feel us out.

It was as if he already knew
what was going on, as if
he'd been returning for ages
to blaspheme the Creek.

26

While the deacons
crawfished into place,
one could scan the bank of faces,
almost hear people calling up Scriptures,
favorite prophets to deliver us.

The sister in the blue crêpe de Chine
sees Joseph released from Potiphar's prison,
and the old man there
with Stetson still on
is remembering Daniel in the lion's den.
Over there Jonah is being spat up . . .
Shadrach, Meshach and Abednego.
Everywhere shields were rising,
going forth against the tree.

A few boys with the story
of David and Goliath
burning their hearts
gathered stones to make war,
aimed to chuck the devil down
into the cloudy waters below,
but Pastor Gamble, an old hand
at this sort of thing, cautioned,
"Leave him be, chillun.
Long as he up there,
we knows where he at."

White Horses

This time
it was only them
being let out
to the damp alfalfa
of landscapes
by Duncanson and Constable,
to celebrate their legs
after a late August shower
before evening's golden web
had disappeared in mist,
turned back
to thunderhead.

Still, amid
the pristine opinions
of crickets and dove,
the spray of rainbow
across the sky
and family venturing forth
to the porch
to choose cloud homes
and watch hydrangeas
lift their burdens
of blue clusters,

it was eerie
how they appeared
on the horizon
single file like a vein
of lightning,
nothing but verb
as they branched out
and circled the valley

trampling dandelion
and clover —
from mane to croup
to fetlock,
every ounce
brighter than stars.

The whole while
seemed so Morphean
the way they moved
in tandem, stirring
those fiery heads
from grazing
for every invisible noise,
and then like
a white tide,
moved for hidden shores
as if answering
some otherworldly call.

Philosophers remind
time and again
that the joys
of metaphor
are best applied
to such events,
to squarely challenge,
as Euripides did,
god and beast
and mystery to come.

But that evening
there wasn't a one of us
who didn't think
of Revelation
in a literal sense,

who didn't wonder
of the red, the black,
the pale horses
yet to come.

Across the distance
our ears imagined
the fugue of hooves
as the last of them
breached the mist
and left us to
a few remaining moments
of verdancy and rainbow,
as they vanished
with a fire
that promised
they'd be back
the first chance
they could.

Whippoorwill

What conundrum tonight
from that reedy fringe
lush with shadows and fluting:
"Chip white oak-a-red oak"
or "Dick married the widow,"
as the elders used to say —
if either of these?

And how is it
that your trill singing
can move me to visions
of concentric rings,
words like *praise* and *calling*,
that even at this stage
after all the notches of meditation
and learning to listen so intently
that my own heartbeat
could almost leave me insane,
I still can't pinpoint your place?

Neither can the fireflies'
bright system of flints
uncover the ventriloquy
beneath layers of stars.
But on wings as soft
as indigo skies
you cruise through your business
of beetles and moths, to
whatever is so urgent
you'd needle us all night
to perceive.

After dusk sometimes,
I'd stray from the child's play
of maypops or dreaming
and off the sandy path
by our house
toward a veil of thickets
to find where you lay.

Perhaps more than once
in orient light,
I stepped harmlessly over
the lichenesque feathers, my foot
barely missing your bristled mouth.

And even now,
pressed near a window screen,
my ear searches for clues
while you riddle into the night
as invisible as faith
in the silvery gardens
of your moon.

Juke

Saturday night. The gravel stretch
beams, crunches, rises in thick clouds
from the string of cars
coming by both routes.
The diamond has cooled down
from a day of scorching grounders
like quarts of beer inside.

A full chalky moon serves
merely as a reminder
of a waiting cue ball. And after
a few cold ones, the boys stop noticing
how bald the green has gotten,
how corners refuse shots
with lots of backspin. By then,
shooters will've honed their englishes
to a warped perfection, swearing more
for the hell of it than anything else
when they blow the 8.

Perhaps tonight, no one gets cut or shot;
perhaps tonight, no one wants to do
a thing besides get loud. Maybe
the men have come just to try
the bump-and-grind girls who
frequent the joint, quaff 90 proof corn
and get high as a Georgia pine.

By two, the haze,
which by twelve is
as smoky as an autumn drizzle,
thins with the dwindling crowd.
As usual, fish fry and crap game
prove shining successes—likewise
the jukebox's appropriate tunes.
Shortly, the old neon flickers out
like a wavering firefly,
closing shop on any leftover dreams,
blessing the last of the dark.

Marigolds

I forget which prize my sister
was selling her flowers for that summer —
perhaps a purse or bracelet
or some other trinket she'd tire of
even before school resumed.

And besides Miss Virginia,
who lived one hill over,
I can't remember
any of her perennial customers
excepting me of course.

Every year the sunny colors
of her seed packets
tricked me
into mining my pockets
for comic book and snow cone money

in the vain desire
that even without a green thumb
I too could raise such buttery pompons.
Nightly I'd dreamt of them
sprouting toward the sky

like magic beanstalks,
that they'd be waiting there
after only one morning,
supple green wands spangled with dew,
ready to snap open like wings

at any moment
into yellows and oranges without end.
Because each time these would be
my first successes, wonderful little worlds
to which I'd given birth,

I mulched and hoed their soil religiously,
possibly watered them to death.
Summer after summer
I prepared for them like newborns:
saving empty packets to use as markers,

predicting the likeliest realms of light,
even finding help
to pronounce genus and family names
for plants that never showed up.
So I'd decided that this gardening

was for the birds.
But that summer when my uncle's retriever
parted our hill's emerald curtain
three times one evening
from some secret nest, each time

with a frail, squirming bunny
in the soft cradle of his mouth
and placed each one at my feet,
and when I'd managed
to keep the strongest of them alive

with alchemies of water and Pet milk
for almost a week
and at last buried them in a cigar box
in a field near our house,
I was crazy for more marigolds.

Again I was willing to sacrifice
any sum of earthly goods
for my sister's golden seeds of hope
to lavishly strew their tomb
and bloom them back to life.

June

On nights like these
as a chorus of hoot owls
convenes just out of sight
in the Rorschach of trees,
a few fireflies
late to find mates
dip through the mood
like chips of neon.

The distant rumble of thunder
nudges a frequent rabbit
slightly lower
in this yard
of delightful neglect
while leaves and curtains
are rustled by
calm omens of rain.

Somewhere in the world
cattleya or bird-of-paradise
may be wafting into screens
but here breezes are draped
in honeysuckle
and trumpet vine.
Here air is crowded
with the twitter
of frogs and crickets,
the random yapping
of a neighbor's feist.

Houses that crackled all day
with the rusty chirp
of hedge clippers,
summer's chords of sparrows
and edgers, kids
springing on trampolines
now simmer like embers.
Glads and day lilies dream
under a street lamp's
alabaster glow.

Sometimes a plane glides
loudly through the indigo
till it vanishes
behind the crown of pines,
till it's again still enough
to consider this universe
of atoms embracing
into flowers and light and rain
for all the Junes that follow.

Midsummer

The rain stops. It's dusk
and the sky is a foreign tangerine;
the only music is huddled doves,
frogs wanting more rain. Mimosas
and roses regain their composure.

Steam rises like a herd
of souls. And just over
the electric next ridge,
a raven-haired gypsy
sends her charms for me.

Haute Cuisine

"As long as we kept carrying him $5,000 dogs,
he was eating good."

All that heaven of cypress knees,
bright darting of damselfly wings,
a flush of egrets along the creek's
ancient sheen, abundant Florida light
shining river sedge and Spanish moss
like brushloads of thalo. Nothing to do
beyond holding sway among tobogganing otters,
mosquitoes twanging like violins, nothing
beyond patrolling shores and shallows
for prized hounds too hot on the trail
of some woodsy aroma to notice
the horrible flower of his mouth.

Twenty years hunters had guessed
their dogs were being pinched by thieves,
while tags moored inside him
as if from soldiers missing in action,
but once only a quarter-mile
from a popular swimming hole,
it was feared his taste could change.

Then came contracted trappers,
all of them seasoned gator catchers,
who found the monster, wrestled him
like Jacob till his indigestion blessed them
with expensive tracking collars, till
the glades were again as safe
as at the end of an old sci-fi movie

where, the evil having been disposed of,
credits roll up over a handsome hero
and his beautiful love interest.

Harpooned and prostrate, all
five hundred pounds of it
across a rusty flatbed, now hardly more
than handbags and loafers —
the broad snout duct-taped shut, belly
slit, that flabby evolution of legs
trussed up behind him
like a holiday feast,
his eyes tangled with confusion
as to why he'd been blamed
for only wanting the very best.

Mowing the Lawn

Funny how
the littlest things
can send you kneeling,
like a twig or dandelion
you bow to retrieve
from near perfect turf.
And while slumped
under the brunt
of afternoon heat
you notice the most common
of worlds,
like a spider
answering its calling,
the tiny bulb of a body
as vivid as bleeding
as it creeps
back and forth
like practicing scales
over the breadth
of its loom.

Don't ask me how it knew
the storm of my blade
had finally passed
or how something so small
had survived a mower
snarling full throttle
through the overdue grass.

Granted, an inky snake
had squirted
dangerously close

but past the cyclone
unharmed, two rusty toads
which I mistook for clods
sidestepped the furious wheels
and even a butterfly
had fluttered
off its bloom
just in the nick
of time.

But here was something
not big as a droplet —
a monster in gnat's clothes —
thriving among streams
of Bermuda confetti,
spinning business as usual
for its keep.

Drained but smiling
I raised myself
in the peace
of completion
wondering what could be
weak enough
for it to snare,
in a realm
where one often becomes
fertile ground
for revelation

and notices symbols
like the tortoise and hare
indicating the mower's
choice of speeds,
where one remembers
that he seldom studies

the slender efficiency
of snakes anymore
or a butterfly's
ice blue wings
settling on pink globes
of bachelor's-button,

where he considers
how many yards
have been cut
at hare's speed
and then only
to get to other jobs,
how in the end
it was the tortoise
who won the race.

Later, in a warm spell
of birds,
I crouched before
the spider's work
amazed at how handily
each sterling
wisp of cable,
by this time as bright
as cathedral glass,
had bound the setting sun.

Ceremony

They wait months
    on a ripe display
        to forge southerly V's,
            wings attuned
                to a solar mood —
          the greenest brant
        knows a world of apexes
      and a cadence fetching
as déjà vu.

Moles

There're days when we too
    do as little as fattening
        among chrysanthemums, when

our lives must seem as mundane,
    and even clothes bind
        like a chamber of dirt.

Yet, on a whim we can
    surface into the potpourri
        of wild pink and jasmine

or drift to the singing of orioles —
    the *joie de vivre*
        a world above

their tithes of scuffing,
    their blind wanderlust
        through pebbles and bulbs.

Fall Song

At the swings,
    beneath a drizzle
        of elm, our eyes would
            mumble our notions.
We'd pause
    to the brief
        flit of wings, toe
            fallen sparks of leaves
till hunger
    at last drove
        all the children
            home, left us
the perfect light.
    There I'd cup
        my hands so gently
            you'd barely know
my need.
    I'd send you
        a little way,
            do without you
as long as I dared —
    then we'd tell each other
        things we'd waited
            all our lives to hear.

Hernando Point

A cool had already begun
hinting an end to summer.
And as days go, this one went:
supplying its daily bread,
a grief synonymous
with the embering world.

Sweeping waves shone
like knives while I
imagined the Atlantis below.

And either these three hadn't heard
about the one who'd drowned
the Sunday before at a dam
just down the road
or for the time being,
gambled the waters appeased.

None of them knew
someone was watching who'd
seen the boy's last splashings,
who'd witnessed his blue body
being hauled in with hooks.

Obviously none of them
had awakened gurgling
from flooded lungs
but dreamt only of
tomorrow's swimming amid
the fiery hallelujahs of fall.

Lively Oracles

What is it then if stones speak
in soft code one to another, if
scarlet, gold and cinnamon leaves
scumble God's message on the hearts
of streams, if wellsprings spool

over their kingdoms of mink
and bream revealing His aim?
What is it when a season's touch
pries a first violet from the scheme
of earth, when a certain air

means the last wink of blooms
should hide like drowsy animals
till the next green blaze —
what then when something that's not
the tongues of a thrush

or jack pines rushed with light
can open the body and change
the course of life? If just once,
there's a stirring that moves
on the blood, someplace where

we wonder who couldn't stay forever,
where we're made to think of swans,
to ask for their perfection, especially
their wings to lift ourselves
as white as the bones of a child.

Blackberry Fools

Devil's shoestrings, walls of woodbine,
snakeskins crumpled like silver code,
barbwire, now and then an angry bull.
We hardly noticed the biting flies.
We took them all on, waded branches,
scrambled down ravines — in early morning;
best of all, in the afternoon;
light forays just before dusk.
We wanted them, like something taboo,
sought them out and kept tabs on
their times of ripening from a strict
inedible red to the lavish black
that bled across trails, plumped
to the dark thimbles that would fill
all our empty lard tins, cookpots
and any Mason jars we could manage.

The earth gave under our load.
This when the world was young
and blinder, or holier, but more.
We always seemed within reach
of something: jeweled birds
that just flitted away in time,
a hive of places we liked believing
no one had ever found. The hills
rang with names and nicknames
as grown-ups shouted for our whereabouts.
This when the sky was as blue
as a trance, when cool welts left
by briers harvesting our arms

meant no more than a necessary pain,
when bushes blazed like dark sayings,
heaving their priestly bait.

Epoch

Slaves to muddy channels,
we prodded crawfish
like impish shepherds to see
them backpedal. It was when

all summer our lips stayed
the burgundy of loganberries,
before we lost our freedom
in that first long kiss.

And when the moon laid limbs out
in dim filigree, knit the landscape
into silhouette, the older folk
sat for awhile and watched

as we stopped and listened to how
they'd also choked Coke bottles
with lightning bugs. Nearby
the wings of birds stumbled

against the blue night — all night
just the wings of birds,
catching and letting go,
bottling light and time.

Raking Leaves

At some point the ritual
becomes so second nature
that one is left free enough
to wonder about such trivia
as the spelling of "leaf,"
how Adam established
an order of vowels.

We spend sweat and fire
on something which good brisk spring winds
would in time send skittering
to the four corners
of the earth.

No, all this effort
has to be about something more
than their withering
from when we knew them
green and sprightly
to the cinnamon spirals of papier-mâché
pooling over a yard,

something more along the lines
of how we feel
about death and dying,
our compulsion to sweep them
out of sight and mind.

The Men's Club Hunt

They came down from Memphis, friends
of my uncle and co-workers of theirs
driving pickups, wearing camouflage coats
gorged with deaths, bird shot or buckshot
depending on the season, armed with
pumps and a few double-barreleds.

They brought speckled bird dogs
or a knot of motley hounds
depending on the season, fifths
of Wild Turkey wrapped in paper bags,
then wandered behind the house
for a ritual of swigs

before starting out. We walked
for hours under a gloomy haze,
me halving their man-steps — for hours
worming through puffs of ragweed,
crunching into sometimes calf-high snow,
watching the best dogs solve networks

of thorns. You could tell the best dogs.
Those were the ones that weren't gun-shy,
that wouldn't wince as shot blazed
right past their heads. They were
the ones that hardly made a sound
while being whipped into shape.

There was a camaraderie in how
the group finished one's whiskey first
before opening another fifth, in how they
traded mysteries of women they'd known
and glanced back to see if I'd grin, the way
they mirrored poor creatures they hunted —

both trying to escape the dangers
of their worlds by the only familiar means.
Behind, I followed the rubies of blood
as they leaked through game bags, the fresh
dangle of trophies, beholding my reflection
in the frozen gaze of a quail's eye.

Firelight

In it are Moses'
burning charge and Pharaoh's hellish plagues,
even God's own eyes
according to Daniel and John,
the orange metaphor

that deacons and church mothers
have felt for ages
shut up in their bones,
a crackling omen
of the fire next time,

the doom of Sodom and Chicago,
Sherman blazing his way
toward the coast,
Joan of Arc,
the witches of Salem

all sizzling and rising
in braids of blue smoke,
a backlog shifting and one
bold comet of bark
tailing through the grate,

Prometheus fleeing
from Olympus, down toward
some cold dark cave,
clutching the blistering embers
of a bright new day.

Landmarks

Talk about cringing
when Sonny heard Siren
in the muddy wash
beneath Baptist Lane —
even when he skinned

to his BVDs,
crab-walked the steep cliff
to the huge culvert's
very tip, it was still
a good thirty-foot dive.

That summer, I knew
we could never last as friends —
I mean, he should've respected
my fear of heights, that brotherhood
of chickens who always toe the line.

Years later, when I heard his woman
had shot him, it was winter, frozen over.
All I cared to think of was us
hunting birds with air rifles, aiming
into a sunburst of pines,

the flinch of a finger
reducing the highest,
gayest of songs into
lumps of bright feathers
hurling toward the cold snowy ground.

Evanescence

We zigzagged like satyrs through the pines
to where a great blue heron
would be mining silver minnows

from the shoal, flung tee shirts
and khakis across branches till the bank
was a launderette of willows.

We were summer fixtures there,
sun-burnished bathers of a pastoral painting,
shuddering the desperate breathing of sex

as we attuned ourselves
with the water's virgin chill.
Even back then, the pond had begun silting up,

thickening with twigs and leaves.
In no time, it seems, nothing was left
but our dry bed of memories,

the countdown of which boys remain,
and somewhere at the back of our splurging,
that knowledge of Eden changing.

Natchez Trace

It seems more of a ballad
than anything else now,
a winding archive
of sun worship and sacrifice,
a passage to souvenirs.

Distant groves boil and shimmer
like murky ghosts
through the rising heat.
The red-tailed hawk
sinks to her perch
like one who has entered a coliseum.

Under the powder blue ceiling,
triumvirates of dizzy buzzards circle
searching for roadkill
not far from where a steely armadillo
lies bloating on the shoulder,
its eyes glazed
with a vision of grubs,
its feet heavenward
like a plump Titan
hefting some invisible load.

Throughout the hush
is a piercing void, that
ethereal chill of history, a siren's
incomprehensible singing.

The Falcon

As we drove past painterly fields of ochre and crimson, under a sky almost cornflower blue, the child in me longed to cry, "Look at the pretty hawk!" as it hovered above breezy grasses, spying for a cue to plummet, but the grownup whispered, "It's so familiar to you." For example, judging by the tail and rapid wing strokes, it wasn't a hawk at all. From that blue and white dispensation of feathers, the blackish brown bars, it looked to be the American variety of peregrine falcon. Ask me how fast it flies, its favorite prey, where it prefers to nest, ask its wingspread, common name, or the color of its eggs. Mind you, there was a time when such a bird could've eclipsed any of my expeditions for poke sallit, persimmons, or what have you, when I would've followed with the lust of an Aztec for the miracle of a feather. Even now, it's still wonder enough for me to slow down till cars behind us pass, to hold me gazing in the rearview mirror while it perches in the ghost of a once sprawling oak.

God's Acre

From the chain of backsliders
that show up each year
just before third Sunday in May
to work the dirt
into cultivated mounds, get rid of
honeysuckle and kudzu, to sweep
and whitewash dusty headstones,
one can feel the weight of blood.

The cemetery floods
with sisters who long ago parted ways
over caches of china
and company sheets,
black sheep cousins, the outside child
people whispered about. Everywhere
an unction of shovels
and joblades labor in a kind
of Protestant Feralia for the good
of common ground.

Toads and spiders stampede
toward the beautiful refuge
of tombs unscathed by duty or love.

Here, even among friends,
there's hardly ever more
than cautious chat of weather,
how tight the soil has grown.
It takes too much to forget
harsh last words, how thin and silent
one can become, too much
not to dwell on heaven or hell,

just to survive till these sparse Sundays
when remnants come with iris and roses,
big yellow and pink Kleenex mums,
when the hard ghosts of living
are buried for awhile
under a covenant of blooms.

A Simpler Optimism

The wood pewee sings at daybreak and at twilight
— *The World Book Encyclopedia*

Sometimes there's a moral
in the most frivolous fact;
and often when there is,
we've known it all along —

just fancy nightfall
as a richer degree of day,
carrying stars, that everyone
may have his own piece of light.

Then, there are birds that sing
both day and night. Maybe
notice how the freer kind
always sees some light.

Savanna

Right before spring, when time came
to burn, the whole family was on
stand-by. The fact that in
nothing flat the flames could hop
their border like Samson's foxes

and swallow up vast chunks
of someone else's place meant
making sure we'd soaked plenty rags.
Once the bone yard of bushes
and grass had caught, there was no

second-guessing the mood of a breeze.
Everything went up in crackling tongues.
It went up like Elijah's offering —
in climbing waves of orange, the smoke
fanning out like a huge black fleece.

There was no way to warn
the napping wood rabbit. One could
only hope the goldfinch found its way.
It was still too early for us
to pick up any parable of life

after death, to make some
connection between circumcision and this.
For us just then, it was hard to see
Daddy's fresh green Beulah, his trees
as anything but stems of fire.

Ephemerida

So much is left to be thought
about the way woods swell
and flush forth green
after drinking April rain, about
the way worlds depart unfledged in death.
Neither the rain nor the green
holds any glad promise
when the center of everything
is an ephemeral cross —
not a savior's cross, not even a thief's
unless the thievery has indeed
been passed down from Paradise,
but perhaps more aptly
a firm rule, hollow and terse.

Such thinking makes rain a somber thing
and rainbows from like views
are nothing more, or slightly more
than transient currents of color
though they hang like lockets
from the neck of heaven, deferred, always brief.
There's little enough time
to read their poems.
Still, half that is spent
in a peculiar compulsion,
trying to translate and elucidate
with clever words without cliché
or merely to copy them
as is from the sky.

Flowers too, like rainbows and rain,
are a fleeing importance.
Bluebonnets, by definition, are low, annual
prairie flowers, purplish and precious to Texas.
By definition means to explain
the matters-of-fact
of matters and facts
paralleling life in its all too concise form —
tangible meanings, abrupt and muffled,
subtracting even more from God's brief gifts.

A fuller rhetoric seems interpretation —
where every noun, every verb
is an unabridged volume.
In such a dictum, bluebonnets are more,
can begin to become
what they were meant to be.
Their blossoms in this way
remain blue but reborn,
are freed to join the dreams
of all who proceed
through the bleary maze,
more different and difficult each time
that everyone might learn again and again
and know that nothing is known.

Not far from anywhere —
for Sirius isn't far, only improbable —
is a place, a pond
or lake where men
strung trotlines now rotten
to catch fish once there.

Now only the warmer months
can cause the water to remember
some of what it was during its dawn.
Equally shallow from middle to edge,
it barely echoes the twinkling
of gangs of lightning bugs
dispensed about as if to patch holes
in the lake's fading memory.

Perhaps the spirits of fish
still quicken remnants of line
when ripples move in soft wind.
Everything listens and recalls
the rich bath of song,
reminisces how frogs boasted
their slick jade skins
atop pastel-petaled lily pads,
and just past the banks
handsome horses galloped red clover slopes.
Down the trail a bit
children chased fence lizards up oaks
and gums till the stout limbs ended.

In infancy, splendor is vast.
Yet splendor also answers a reaper,
thus bidding seekers
to sharpen every sense,
to look beneath the scummed surface
of any dying lake.

Down inside the lively mud
an order of nymph prepares
for a single day of sight.
It will emerge mature, mouthless,
without stomach or desire for food.
Drawn in droves by the essence of light
they expel exit with entry,
dancing and mating in midair.

O fragile May fly,
you who must realize better than most
the worth of things,
reveal to all who grope for reason
what should be done
before the hour is up
and our sun finally descends.

Way of Life

After twenty years, judgment returned
like an anniversary
in the same lean absence
of fruiting vines, the same
bristling gloom as before,
working under clouds
of early mist at first
and on through dark
till there was no crunch of traveling,
nothing more than that glassy clicking,

a Pleistocene solitude,
all night the groaning and snapping
of branches and trunks giving in,
till no sights or motion
were left to one
but his tunneling dream
of the great owl locked fast
in its gnarled hollow,
a vole nestling in thatch.

Hour upon seemingly endless hour
the records fell
cocooning us in ice
till at last by morning,
freezing rain and sleet
had become pendulums
of white flakes
drifting over evergreens,
burying woodpiles and roads.

Fallen power lines and glacial debris
would again make the news'
rundown of disasters, perhaps
leave those elsewhere,
under the warm sunbow
of their morning,
wondering how we could cope.

What we share in this world
are the beautiful depths
of human illogic
that would have us trade places
with a suffering lover, cause us
to momentarily forget
that going on is seldom, if ever,
the result of happiness returning,
anything more than hope.

We rise for what we have left:
swatches of buntings perched
and preening, stars of embers
that need to be stirred,
gardens of brilliant drooping, some
brave soul's template of tracks.

Dealate

Even before some power in the thorax
pinches up that crisp tissue of wings,
the trinity of their bodies
is continually being printed
with obsessions for buoyancy,
how to do it when at last
they emerge Mars and Venus, erupt
like a frenzy of tulle toward heaven
in their one mating flight
where they obey a primeval map
for abdomens and legs, in what
mustn't ever freelance into anything
exotic, but be kept normal and precise.

We all know about Lucifer,
or Adam and Eve for that matter,
how they became dewinged as it were,
but I either heard or read somewhere
that all of us were perfect once,
before we were plucked from among
the bright environs of Pleiades and Orion
and made flesh for our stabs
at the mystery of purpose.

And what if we are no less
than seraphim displaced, trudging along
the sins of the fathers,
through exams in relentlessness,
searching for a way back to God?

Even a fall from angel to ant
shouldn't seem so implausible
when one considers the queens
are sufficiently carnal in that one brief moment
to be confined for life, then
tumble back toward scrub and dirt,
into their labyrinth of cellars
for the proliferation of heirs
to resume the work of the earth.

About the Author

Claude Wilkinson was born in Memphis, Tennessee and grew up on a farm in northwest Mississippi. He has taught in the English departments of a number of colleges and universities. Over the years his poems have appeared in numerous journals and anthologies. Also a visual artist, his drawings and paintings have been featured in exhibitions at the African American Museum, Carnegie Center for Arts and History, Cottonlandia Museum, Tennessee Valley Art Center, and Tupelo Artist Guild Gallery, among many other invitational, juried, and solo shows. He lives in Nesbit, Mississippi.